FLYING ON THE WINGS OF THE EAGLE

"The Christian Eagle"

EMMANUEL OKEREKE

Flying on the Wings of the Eagle
"The Christian Eagle"
By: Emmanuel Okereke

Cover Picture: Jazzy Kitty Publications
Logo Designs by Andre M. Saunders and Jess Zimmerman
Editor: Anelda L. Attaway

© 2020 Emmanuel Okereke
ISBN 978-1-7349014-0-5
Library of Congress Control Number: 2020906768

All rights reserved. This book is protected under the copyright laws of the United States of America and the copyright laws of Ghana. This book may not be copied or reprinted for commercial gain or profit. The use of short quotations or occasional page copying for personal or group study is permitted and encouraged. Permission will be granted upon request. Unless otherwise identified, scripture quotations are from the King James Version of the Bible. For Worldwide Distribution, available in Paperback. Printed in the United States of America. Published by Jazzy Kitty Greetings Marketing & Publishing, LLC. dba Jazzy Kitty Publications utilizing Microsoft Publishing Software.

FOREWORD

Understanding these great truths will transform your life and encourage you to fly high as God expects you to. That is why you need to encounter this great book written by this great servant of God Bishop Emmanuel Okereke.

As you read through the pages of this revealing book, you are awakened to who you are in Christ, what God has made you and what you are to do to attain the level. As an eagle-like believer we are to mount up with great power to create impact and effect where we are to the glory of God. I believe God is waiting for us to rise to the occasion and to release these great powers that are within us.

As you read this revealing book, I pray there will be a great stirring up in you and the momentum that will cause you to mount up and be effective to create impact.

Bishop Okereke has given us these great truths to help us; read it with your Spirit and an open mind then get ready to soar up to God's glory.

Bishop (Dr.) Akwasi Agyemang (Jnr)

Presiding Bishop

(Word Impact Center, Ghana)

ACKNOWLEDGMENTS

My first acknowledgement goes to the Almighty God for the wisdom, grace, and guidance. He has given me the authority to write this book and the obedience to finish it.

Also, my sincere acknowledgement also goes to the following people: My wife, Annie Ogba Okereke and my children for standing with me.

Also, to Miss Robin Brooks for all the support she has given me with the publication of this book and for standing with me in my ministry.

Lastly, Anelda Attaway CEO and Publisher of Jazzy Kitty Publications, thank you for assisting me with the publication of my book and your guidance throughout the process.

DEDICATION

First, I humbly dedicate this book to the Almighty for the wisdom and strength to write this book.

Also, to all Pastors, Evangelist, Prophets, Apostles in the Lord, and to all Christian Leaders.

Lastly but not least, to my wife, family, and to all members of the Faith Authority Chapel International.

TABLE OF CONTENTS

INTRODUCTION..i

CHAPTER 1 – The Bird Eagle...01
    The Parts of the Eagle..01
    The Claws 03
    The Beak 04

CHAPTER 2 – God as an Eagle...06
    You as an Eagle..07
    Similarities Between the Christian and the Eagle.......................07
    7 Principles of an Eagle – Dr. Myles Monroe............................09

CHAPTER 3 – The Wings of the Eagle Christian 22
    The Wings of the Eagle Christian...22
    Faith as a Wing of the Eagle Christian 23
    Love as a Wing of the Eagle Christian 27
    Mounting up with Wings 25

CHAPTER 4 – The Power of Faith...27
    Faith Comes by Hearing the Word 27
    Developing a Strong Wing of Faith 28
    Waiting Upon the Lord 29
    Putting Your Faith to Work 30

CHAPTER 5 – Power of Patience...32
    Catching a Prey 32
    Patience is Endurance 33

CHAPTER 6 – The Training of the Eaglet.....................................27
    Developing a Strong Strength of Faith 37
    Using Your Faith to Deal with Challenges................................39

TABLE OF CONTENTS

The Eagle and the Storm 39
CHAPTER 7 – The Conclusion 42
ABOUT THE AUTHOR 43
ABOUT THE BOOK 45

INTRODUCTION

As the Bible declares in **Isaiah 40:31** "But those who wait on the Lord shall renew their strength; they shall mount up with wings like eagles, they shall run and not be weary, they shall walk and not faint. (NKJV)

Every born-again believer is considered to be an eagle, and as eagles, the Eagle-God created us as eagles to reign in every sphere of life. The eagle is a great and wonderful bird, as the king of all birds it has lessons to teach us if we are going to reign as Christians in this life.

The Bible declares in **Revelation 5:10** "And have made us kings and priests to our God; and we may reign on the earth." As eagles, as kings, and priests, we are created to reign in every aspect of life. Our dwelling is not on this earth, it is in the heavenly places.

The eagle is the king of birds, and it flies higher than any other bird, and soars higher base on the strength of the wings, without wings it cannot soar. There are about sixty (60) species of the eagle bird in the whole world. So, every eagle Christian has two wings on which he or she soars higher in every area of life. As eagle Christians, we are to be the head and not the tail, above and not below.

CHAPTER 1

The Bird Eagle

Deuteronomy 28:49 [49]The LORD will bring a nation against you from afar, from the end of the earth, as swift as the eagle flies, a nation whose language you will not understand. (NKJV)

The bird eagle is a very interesting bird; it is the king of all the birds. It is the master of the sky; it is the only bird liken to God. The largest, including the Harpy Eagle and the Philippine Eagle, can weigh more than 20 pounds and have wings that spread eight feet across. Using their massive, sharp talons, these giants can kill and carry off prey as large as deer and monkeys.

Exodus 19:4 [4]'You have seen what I did to the Egyptians, and how I bore you on eagles' wings and brought you to Myself. (NKJV)

It is also likening to Jesus Christ. Jesus Christ has four features, as declared in **Revelation 4:7** [7]And the first beast was like a lion, and the second beast like a calf, and the third beast had a face as a man, and the fourth beast was like a flying eagle. (KJV) From the above scripture Jesus Christ has four features, the eagle is also attributed to the Christian. Jesus Christ is first of all a Man, a Lion, a calf, and an eagle. All the features of the eagle and its behavior can be attributed to the eagle Christian.

The Parts of the Eagle:

Almost all the parts of the eagle have significant meaning and can be attributed to the Christian. The major parts of the eagle are the head, eyes, wings, claws, and the beak. The following are the meaning of the parts of the eagle:

- **The Head of Eagle:**

The head of the eagle represent leadership. The eagle is a leadership bird, and it is a lone ranger bird, the eagle is always leading. As eagle Christians we are called to take the lead and not to take the least, to stay ahead and not behind. Leadership is a lonely call and ministry. Every Christian is a potential leader.

- **The Eyes of Eagle:**

The eyes of the eagle is made up of a powerful lenses which enables it to see an object or a prey from 200 to 300 meters away, Eagles' eyes are extremely powerful, having up to 3.6 times human acuity for the martial eagle, which enables them to spot potential prey from a very long distance.[2] It is able to see an object which is beyond the human eyes. And it is able to target its prey from a very high altitude and it doesn't miss its prey. The eye of the eagle represents the eye of the prophet, and it represents the Christian's ability to see into the realm of the spirit to know what the Lord is saying. The Lord has given every Christian the ability to foresee the evil of the enemy and to escape from them as an eagle. It also represents vision, the eagle is a bird of vision, and every Christian is empowered by the Holy Spirit to have a vision for his or her life, for where there is none that person will go astray.

Proverbs 22:3 [3]A prudent man foresees evil and hides himself, but the simple pass on and are punished. (NKJV)

Proverbs 29:18 [18]Where there is no revelation, the people cast off restraint; but happy is he who keeps the law. (NKJV)

© **The Wings of Eagle:**

Revelation 12:14 [14]And two wings of a great eagle were given to the woman, so that she might fly into the wilderness, into her place, where she is nourished for a time and times and half a time, from the serpent's face. The eagle has two wings and the strength of the eagle is in its wings called talons. The majestic eagle with its powerful and graceful wings, it can soar through the sky and cause traffic to stop on the side of a road for anything but modest picture. It is a symbol of power, strength, and thievery. Surprised? You'll be interested to know that there are many things that you might not know about the eagle. The woman in the above scripture refers to the Christian church; every Christian is supposed to have two wings in order to fly higher in the things of the spirit. We are expected by God to soar higher in the spirit. The wing of the Eagle-Christian refers to his or her Faith and Patience (Love). (Hebrews 6:12)

Hebrews 6:12 [12]That you do not become sluggish but imitate those who through faith and patience inherit the promises. (NKJV)

The Claws:

Daniel 4:33 [33]The same hour was the thing fulfilled upon Nebuchadnezzar: and he was driven from men, and did eat grass as oxen, and his body was wet with the dew of heaven, till his hairs were grown like eagles' feathers, and his nails like birds' claws.

The claw of the bird refers to the pointed nails of a bird, it is also known in the Bible as hoof. This is the part of the body of the eagle that it uses to scrap the ground; the eagle uses this part of its body to raise big objects and big things, some which are usually bigger than the eagle itself. The eagle uses its claws to possess and pick what belongs to it, the Holy Spirit by revelation made me to understand that the claws of the eagle-Christian refers to the feet of the believer.

Joshua 14:9 [9] And Moses sware on that day, saying, Surely the land whereon thy feet have trodden shall be thine inheritance, and thy children's forever, because thou hast wholly followed the LORD my God. The believer as an eagle possesses with his or her feet, the Christian as an eagle must be able to lay hold on his or her possession and take it by force.

The Beak:

The beak, bill, or rostrum is an external anatomical structure of birds which is used for eating and for grooming, manipulating objects, killing prey, fighting, probing for food, courtship and feeding young.

Like all birds of prey, eagles have very large hooked for tearing flesh from their prey. They also use their beak to eat up the prey they tear into pieces. They also use their beak to fight and killing preys and feeding their young ones.

The mouth of the eagle - Christian must not speak ill or negative but must always be seasoned with salt.

Isaiah 50:4 (NKJV) [4][The Servant of God says] The Lord God has given Me the tongue of the learned, that I should know how to speak a word in season to him who is weary. He awakens Me morning by morning; He awakens My ear To hear as the learned [as one who is taught The mouth of the believer must always speak positive and encouraging words. The believer must learn to speak faith.

2 Timothy 4:2 [2]Herald and preach the Word! Keep your sense of urgency [stand by, be at hand and ready], whether the opportunity seems to be favorable or unfavorable. [Whether it is convenient or inconvenient, whether it is welcome or unwelcome, you as preacher of the Word are to show people in what way their lives are wrong]. And convince them, rebuking and correcting, warning and urging and encouraging them, being unflagging and inexhaustible in patience and teaching.

The mouth of the believer must always preach Jesus Christ and wins souls for Jesus Christ. The mouth of the believer must always declare life to the people. The eagle can destroy or tear the head of a serpent into pieces, so with our mouth we overcome the work of Satan.

CHAPTER 2

God as an Eagle

Deuteronomy 32:11-12 [11]As an eagle stirs up its nest, Hovers over its young, spreading out its wings, taking them up, carrying them on its wings,

[12]So the LORD alone led him, and there was no foreign god with him. (NKJV)

- **Exodus 19:4** [4]'You have seen what I did to the Egyptians, and how I bore you on eagles' wings and brought you to Myself. (NKJV)
- The eagle is the main symbol of the Almighty God, when you see the eagle in the Bible it represents God in various forms.
- **God as Leader** - As a leader eagles flock alone, just as God flocks alone, two eagles never flock together, so the leadership journey is a lonely journey and so God is leader.
- **God as a Father** - God's strong and loving care for His people. (Exodus 19:40)
- **God as a Great and Powerful King** - Ezekiel 17:3, Revelation 8:13. The eagle is a symbol of strength, 'rulership' and sovereignty is the king of all bird. Eagles represent sovereignty and supremacy. How fitting is this since God is the *real* ruler of kings and presidents. Daniel. 2:20-21, 5:18-21, Proverbs 8:15-16, Romans 13:1-2 (voices.yahoo.com/**the-eagle-symbolism-gods**-nature-5225773.h by Jack Wellman - in 216 Google+ circles)
- As the renovating and quickening influences of the spirit of God. (Hosea 8:1)
- But they also represent self-sacrifice. And during times of food

shortages, an eagle will tear off part of its own flesh and blood to prevent it's young from starving to death. Even to the point of one of the mate's own death. I see the relationship between the Father and Jesus (tearing of His own flesh and blood to save us from death). voices.yahoo.com/**the-eagle-symbolism-gods-**nature-5225773.h by Jack Wellman-in 216 Google +circles)

You as an Eagle:

But they that wait upon the LORD shall renew *their* strength; they shall mount up with wings as eagles; they shall run, and not be weary; and they shall walk, and not faint. (Isaiah 40:31)

There is a popular saying in Ga, *"A crab does not give birth to a bird,"* what that proverb mean, it means a crab will never give birth to a crab. So, God who is an eagle will surely give to an eagle, and not a chicken. As the Bible says in Psalms 82:6, I have said, Ye *are* gods; and all of you *are* children of the Most High.

Then if God is an eagle then you as a child of God, you are an eaglet, and you must carry the qualities of an eagle. This means that if you are a child of God then, you must carry the qualities and character of God. Herein is our love made perfect, that we may have boldness in the day of judgment: because as He is, so are we in this world. (1 John 4:17)

Similarities Between the Christian and the Eagle:

1. The Basic Gist of The Eagle Analogy

The first thing you need to know about eagles so you can fully understand what the basic gist of this analogy is all about is exactly how they are able to fly, with most of it being on how they are able to **soar** without actually flapping their wings.

I am sure most of you have seen videos and documentaries of eagles being caught on video soaring high up in the sky without actually flapping their wings.

Their wings are spread straight out and they are literally soaring with perfect ease on the wind currents. Eagles are born with big and heavy wings, and part of the survival mechanism they are born with is that they have to learn how to fly without actually flapping their big wings.

They must learn how to do this in order to conserve energy. Eagles can literally die if they expend too much energy flapping their wings during flight as versus soaring without flapping their wings.

As a result, what eagles must learn to do very early on in order to be able to soar without flapping their wings, is to wait for what are called **wind thermals** to come up on them. A wind thermal is a big gust of wind that will rise from the atmosphere.

Sometimes eagles will remain perched for days before they can catch a good, strong, wind thermal, where they can then launch onto it and combine a mixture of flying and soaring on that strong wind thermal to get them to where they want to go.

Now here is the basic gist of this whole analogy. Lock this into your memory banks, as God is giving us a very powerful analogy on how eagles basically fly and soar on these wind thermals.

Bottom line: If we do not have enough faith and patience in God to take flight on the Holy Spirit in order to be led and empowered by Him for service to the Lord, then nothing will ever happen.

We will forever stay perched, and we will never fulfill the divine destiny that God has already planned out for our lives before we were even born into our mother's womb.

The eagle has to take that big leap off the edge of the cliff in order to be able to fly and soar on those wind thermals.

If the eagle does not take flight on those wind thermals when they do come up on him, he will forever stay perched and he will die on the cliff due to starvation.

In the same way, if we do not take flight on the Holy Spirit and the divine call that God has placed on our lives, our lives will perish right before our very eyes, as the Bible tells us that God's people will perish without having His specific vision for their lives.

2. Eagles are Master Fliers

As a result of being able to learn how to fly on those strong wind thermals, eagles are considered **master fliers.** They can fly to heights that no other bird can. They have been seen flying as high as some of our airplanes fly.

If eagles have to be careful not to expend too much energy in flapping their wings because of their size and weight, then how can they fly as high as some our modern-day airplanes? The answer is in their ability and skill to ride and fly on these strong wind thermals. Eagles are friend to the storm as a believer you must be a friend to the storm and must learn to take advantage of it to get to level you get to in life.

This is why you see eagles literally soaring at times on these wind thermals, with their wings being spread straight out and no flapping being done.

In the same way, we as Christians can learn how to be master fliers by learning how to be led by the Holy Spirit on a daily basis.

Just like eagles depend on these strong wind thermals to take them to heights that no other bird can fly to – in the same way we can be taken to heights that we may have never dreamed possible if we will just learn how to be led be the Holy Spirit on a daily basis.

Just think how much more good fruit we could produce, and how much more we could accomplish for the Lord in this lifetime if we could all learn how to be really led by the Holy Spirit on a daily basis, and how to really walk with His power and anointing flowing through us.

Again, this is something that can be learned if you are open and willing to be taught by the Lord on how to do this on a daily basis. It is the job of the Holy Spirit Himself to teach you how to be personally led and empowered by Him so you can fully accomplish everything that the Lord has set out for you to do for Him in this life.

3. Eagles are Master Fisherman

Eagles are also considered master fisherman. They are very good in locking in on their prey and then swooping down to catch them.

How many times have you seen videos where an eagle will swoop down on a body of water and pick up a fish swimming near the surface with perfect ease and accuracy and catching them on the very first attempt. They are **absolute masters** at hunting down and catching their prey, whether that prey be on land or in the water.

Just as eagles are considered to be master fisherman with how they can catch fish in water – we, as Christians, have been called by the Lord to be **"fishers of men,"** just like Jesus and the apostles were at the very beginning of the New Testament. Our number one job in this life is to try and get as many people saved as we possibly can.

Personal evangelism within our own circle of influence is something that each and every Christian can do for the Lord, and it is something that we should always keep our radars up for – as you never know when the Holy Spirit will move on you to lead you to someone He will want you to witness to, whether it be someone you might know or a complete total stranger.

4. Eagles Fly Alone

Though eagles will mate for life, for the most part you will always see them flying alone in the skies.

As Christians, we are all part of the body of Christ, where the little finger is just as important as the big toe.

However, the Bible also tells us that many are called but few are chosen. I believe this verse is referring to our calls in the Lord, not to our personal salvation in Him.

What this verse is telling us is that many of the people God is calling are not being chosen for various reasons.

What this means is that at times you may feel totally alone, depending on the type of calling that God has placed on your life and exactly where you are at in the development of that calling.

David was alone when he took on Goliath. No one else would step on the battlefield with him when he took on that evil blasphemous giant.

Peter was alone when he stepped out of the boat to walk on water, as the Bible says that the rest of the apostles were too scared to try and do it on their own. Moses was all by himself for 40 years in the backside of the desert before God called him out to deliver the Israelites from Egypt.

David was hiding out in caves from Saul for quite a number of years before he was finally called out to become the greatest king of Israel.

At times, you may feel totally isolated and alone at the spot where God may have you at.

When you are in these kinds of dry times and seasons with the Lord, just keep pressing forward and flying alone like the eagle does – and sooner or later God will bring you forth into the heart of your call where everyone will then see you and work with you on the call that God has placed on your life.

5. Eagles Live on Higher Ground

For the most part, eagles will always be found living on some type of higher ground. As Christians, we are already living on higher ground as compared to the rest of the world as a result of who we are in Christ. Living on higher is walking in the Spirit, and we are called to live and walk in the Spirit.

We are now born-again children of the Most High God. We are now kings and priests of the Lord. We now have the Holy Spirit, along His power and knowledge residing on the inside of us to help lead us, sanctify us, and empower us so we can all be used by the Lord in a mighty way for ministry. This is why the Lord is calling all of us to stay in the world, but not to be an actual part of the world.

In other words, we are to be in the world, but not of the world. We are to keep ourselves separate from the corruption, pollution, vices, and sins of this world so God can keep us on His straight and narrow road for the rest of our earthly lives.

We live on this higher ground as a result of our position in Jesus. And we always need to keep reminding ourselves that we are living on this higher ground, as the world will always do everything it can to try and drag us down into their lower way of living.

6. Eagles are Extremely Bold, Courageous, and Powerful

Another very powerful trait of the eagle is that they are very bold, courageous, and powerful. Eagles have literally been seen engaging with poisonous snakes and tearing their heads off with their beak.

They have been seen going right through major storm clouds, where most birds will fly away and hide in safety until the storm has passed.

As we have stated numerous times in some of the articles in our spiritual warfare section, God is calling all of us to become good and mighty soldiers of Jesus Christ.

He is asking all of us to put on His armor and to engage with demons and to cast them out of people when necessary. Just like the eagle has no fear of any man, beast, or snake – in the same way we should have no fear of any demonic spirit or any evil human being since we all have God Himself totally on our side.

The Bible tells us that greater is He that is in us than he who is in the world. David perfectly proved that point when he took out Goliath with one perfectly, well-placed blow.

Just like the eagle is the most powerful and feared bird in the sky – in the same way God the Father can personally raise you up to be a mighty and courageous soldier for Him so you can do great and mighty exploits in the calling that He has personally placed on your life.

7. Eagles are Considered Majestic

Due to the way eagles look and act, many people consider them almost majestic and invincible. They seem to have a look of royalty about them.

In the same way, we, as Christians, have this same air of royalty about us since we are now considered kings and priests of the Lord due to the sacrifice that Jesus has personally made for all of us with His death on the cross.

This majestic royalty that we now have operating through us all comes direct from Jesus. It does not come directly from us, or any of the good works that we may have done to-date for the Lord. It all comes to us as a direct result of Jesus dying on the cross for all of our sins.

Only the blood that Jesus has personally shed for each one of us on the cross is what makes us kings and priests before Him, lest we all get puffed up with our own pride and arrogance, thinking this was all of our own doing and making.

8. Eagles are Faithful for Life

Once eagles' mate with their partners, they will stay true and loyal to that other eagle for life. In the same way, once God leads us to the mate that He will want us to marry in this life, He will expect us to stay true, loyal, and faithful to that mate literally to the day we die.

In this day and age, where 50% of all marriages are still failing and ending up in divorce, this is a tall order for many to stay faithful to their spouses.

God expects all of us to honor our vows and commitments made at the wedding altar. God takes marriage and the vows that come with it very, very seriously, and it is nothing to be trifled with or taken for granted once you hit a few minor speed bumps in the marriage.

The Holy Spirit is the Helper and Counselor, and He can help heal any hurts or misgivings that may have occurred in the marriage if you will just learn how to open yourself up to Him and allow Him to work in whatever state your marriage may be in.

9. Eagles Are Very Patient

Another very interesting quality that eagles have is that they are very patient. Documentary film crews have filmed eagles spotting rabbits they will target as prey.

Once the rabbit senses the danger, he will then go hiding in a hole, sometimes for as long as an hour or two before he finally comes back out.

The eagle will then wait for that hour or two until the rabbit finally comes back out again. And once he does, the eagle will then swoop down and catch him within seconds. As a result of his patience, the eagle will then be rewarded with a big fat meal.

In the same way, we all need the patience of the eagle, especially in the type of world we now live in with everything being done at breakneck speed and people's fuses being shortened as a result of all of the high stress that we are forced to live under.

This is why one of the **9 fruits of the Holy Spirit** is the fruit of patience, as we all need His patience operating through us so we can weather the storm clouds of this turbulent life.

10. The Eagle Has Two Sets of Eyes:

Another very fascinating quality that eagles have is that they have two sets of eyes. The first set is their natural eye which they have when they are in a resting mode.

However, when they start to take flight on these strong wind thermals, they have a second eye that comes in on them. This second eye then enables them to fly on these strong wind thermals without damaging their original eye.

This second eye is also used when they are seen flying through actual storm clouds. The heavy winds from a storm cloud could easily damage their normal natural eye, and this second eye gives them a protective covering as they are navigating through these heavy storm clouds.

As Christians, we also have two sets of eyes operating in us. The first set is our normal natural eye which we use to see the natural world in which we live in. However, we also have a second set of eyes and that is the eyes of the Holy Spirit.

Since we all have the Holy Spirit living on the inside of us, we also have His eyes available to us at times to see things from His perspective.

As you start to draw closer to the Lord in your own personal relationship with Him, there will be times that He will allow you to **"see"** things as He sees them. You will start **"seeing"** what certain Scripture verses may mean. You will start to **"see"** what the real truth is in many of the matters of your own personal life.

When this starts to occur, this is the Holy Spirit Himself allowing you to see things through His eyes, not your eye. This is highly supernatural event when it starts to occur.

It is God Himself literally allowing you to see things from His point of view and perspective. The Bible says that the truth will set you free. But you first have to see what that truth is before it can start to set you free.

This is why we all need the eyes of the Holy Spirit operating in us, so we can start to see what the real truth is on many of the different matters and issues in our own personal lives.

Just like the eagle needs his two sets of eyes in order to be able to live and survive in this world, in the same way we need both our natural eyes and the eyes of the Holy Spirit operating in us so we can properly work and function for the Lord in this life.

Eagles Have Contrasting Color Patterns–Noticeable from a Distance many of the creatures God has created have color patterns that blend in with their natural surroundings so as to protect them from other predators.

However, not so with the eagle. The American bald eagle has dark brown skin with a white colored head. As a result of this contrasting color pattern, they can easily be seen from quite a distance.

I know this may be stretching this analogy a bit, but I believe that the dark skin of the eagle lines up with our flesh colored skins, and the white color on the head and face of the eagle line up with the presence and power of the Holy Spirit living in us. In other words, it is symbolic of the anointing that we have operating in us through the Holy Spirit.

People who walk with a very strong anointing from the Lord are very noticeable from a distance. You can **"see"** the anointing of God all over them. You can **"see"** the manifest presence of the Holy Spirit in the form of a transparent glow radiating out of their faces.

These people have developed very strong personal relationships with the Lord over a number of years and they are walking very close with Him in working out their own personal calls for Him in this life.

Just like the eagle stands out in his environment as a result of his might, prowess, and contrasting color pattern in the animal kingdom – in the same way, highly anointed Christians also stand out in their surroundings due to the presence and power of God Almighty Himself radiating out of them.

Jesus Himself has told us in His Word that He is our light, and that once we have His light shining through us, that we are not to try and hide it underneath the table.

We are to let His light shine through us so we can reach the rest of the world with His message of eternal salvation.

7 Principles of an Eagle – Dr. Myles Monroe:

Principle 1

Eagles fly alone at high altitude and not with sparrows or other small birds. No other bird can get to the height of the eagle. Stay away from sparrows and ravens. Eagles fly with Eagles.

Principle 2

Eagles have strong vision. They have the ability to focus on something up to five kilometers away. When an eagle sites his prey, he narrows his focus on it and set out to get it. No matter the obstacles, the eagle will not move his focus from the prey until he grabs it.

Have a vision and remain focused no matter what the obstacle and you will succeed.

Principle 3

Eagles do not eat dead things. They feed only on fresh prey. Vultures eat dead animals, but eagles will not.

Be careful with what you feed your eyes and ears with, especially in movies and on TV. Steer clear of outdated and old information. Always do your research well.

Principle4

Eagles love the storm. When clouds gather, the eagles get excited. The eagle uses the storm's wind to lift it higher. Once it finds the wind of the storm, the eagles uses the raging storm to lift him above the clouds. This gives the eagle an opportunity to glide and rest its wings. In the meantime, all the other birds hide in the leaves and branches of the trees. We can use the storms of life to rise to greater heights. Achievers relish challenges and use them profitably.

Principle 5

The Eagle tests before it trusts. When a female eagle meets a male and they want to mate, she flies down to earth with the male pursuing her and she picks a twig. She flies back into the air with the male pursuing her.

Once she has reached a height high enough for her, she lets the twig fall to the ground and watches it as it falls. The male chases after the twig. The faster it falls, the faster he chases it. He has to catch it before it falls to the ground. He then brings it back to the female eagle.

The female eagle grabs the twig and flies to a higher altitude and then drops the twig for the male to chase. This goes on for hours, with the height increasing until the female eagle is assured that the male eagle has mastered the art of catching the twig which shows commitment. Then and only then, will she allow him to mate with her. Whether in private life or in business, one should test commitment of people intended for partnership.

Principle 6

When ready to lay eggs, the female and male eagle identify a place very high on a cliff where no predators can reach. The male flies to earth and picks thorns and lays them on the crevice of the cliff, then flies to earth again to collect twigs which he lays in the intended nest. He flies back to earth and picks thorns laying them on top of the twigs. He flies back to earth and picks soft grass to cover the thorns. When this first layering is complete the male eagle runs back to earth and picks more thorns, lays them on the nest; runs back to get grass it on top of the thorns, then plucks his feathers to complete the nest. The thorns on the outside of the nest protect it from possible intruders. Both male and female eagles participate in raising the eagle family. She lays the eggs and protects them; he builds the nest and hunts. During the time of training the young ones to fly, the mother eagle throws the eaglets out of the nest. Because they are scared, they jump into the nest again.

Next, she throws them out and then takes off the soft layers of the nest, leaving the thorns bare When the scared eaglets again jump into the nest, they are pricked by thorns. Shrieking and bleeding, they jump out again this time wondering why the mother and father who love them so much are torturing them. Next, mother eagle pushes them off the cliff into the air. As they shriek in fear, father eagle flies out and catches them up on his back before they fall and brings them back to the cliff. This goes on for some time until they start flapping their wings. They get excited at this newfound knowledge that they can fly.

The preparation of the nest teaches us to prepare for changes; the preparation for the family teaches us that active participation of both partners leads to success; the being pricked by the thorns tells us that sometimes being too comfortable where we are may result into our not experiencing life, not progressing, and not learning at all. The thorns of life come to teach us that we need to grow, get out of the nest, and live on. We may not know it but the seemingly comfortable and safe haven may have thorns. The people who love us do not let us languish in sloth but push us hard to grow and prosper. Even in their seemingly bad actions they have good intentions for us.

Principle 7

When an Eagle grows old, his feathers become weak and cannot take him as fast as he should. When he feels weak and about to die, he retires to a place far away in the rocks. While there, he plucks out every feather on his body until he is completely bare. He stays in this hiding place until he has grown new feathers, then he can come out. We occasionally need to shed off old habits & items that burden us without adding to our lives. (7 principles of an eagle-Dr. Myles Monroe, http://sharelife.wordpress.com/2007/08/22/7-principles-of-an-eagle-dr-myles-monroe/)

CHAPTER 3

The Wings of the Eagle Christian

Hebrews 6:12 [12]That ye be not slothful, but followers of them who through faith and patience inherit the promises.

But they that wait upon the LORD shall renew their strength; they shall mount up with wings as eagles; they shall run, and not be weary; and they shall walk, and not faint. (Isaiah 40:31)

Hebrews 11:1 [11]Now faith is the substance of things hoped for, the evidence of things not seen.

Just as the eagle has two wings and flies on both winds, so is the eagle Christian. The eagle as compared to the eagle Christian has two wings. From the above scripture the Bible says they that wait upon the Lord shall renew their strength, this means that the eagle Christian derives his or her strength from the lord, the Lord is the strength of the believer, and he renews his strength daily by waiting on the Lord. The Bible says that the believer shall mount up with wings after receiving strength. The wings of the eagle are what carries the eagle into the air, so the eagle Christian also rises and fly in the things of the spirit by the wings of faith and patience.

The Wings of the Eagle Christian:

From the above scripture the eagle Christian does three things, he walks, runs and flies. The wings of the eagle Christian are faith and patience which represents love. Therefore, the wings of the eagle Christian are faith and love.

Hebrews 6:12 [12]That ye be not slothful, but followers of them who through faith and patience inherit the promises.

From the above scripture we should imitate those who have gone ahead of us in the Christian faith, those are old eagles who have made it in their faith walk. How they succeeded spiritually, it took faith and patience which is love, to succeed.

Faith as a Wing of the Eagle Christian:

Hebrews 11:6 [6]But without faith *it is* impossible to please *him:* for he that cometh to God must believe that he is, and *that* he is a rewarder of them that diligently seek him.

Hebrews 11:1 [1]Now faith is the substance of things hoped for, the evidence of things not seen.

Romans 1:17 [17]For therein is the righteousness of God revealed from faith to faith: as it is written, The just shall live by faith.

The Christian walk takes faith, without faith the Christian will not be able to soar in the things of the spirit. In actual fact the Bible says (Hebrews 11:2) that by it (faith and patience) our elders (our predecessors) to obtain a good report. The Christian race takes faith to live. Even the Bible call Christianity as 'The faith.' Faith is main key to succeed in the things spirit, everything spiritual miracle is possible by faith, so if you want to fly as an eagle Christian you must understand what faith is and how it works.

Love as a Wing of the Eagle Christian:

1 Corinthians 13:13 [13]And so faith, hope, love abide [faith–conviction and belief respecting man's relation to God and divine things; hope–joyful and confident expectation of eternal salvation; love–true affection for God and man, growing out of God's love for and in us], these three; but the greatest of these is love.

Hebrews 6:12 In order that you may not grow disinterested and become [spiritual] sluggards, but imitators, behaving as do those who through faith (by their leaning of the entire personality on God in Christ in absolute trust and confidence in His power, wisdom, and goodness) and by practice of patient endurance and waiting are [now] inheriting the promises.

The second wing of the eagle believer is love, without love the believer cannot soar in the things of the spirit. From the above scripture the Bible says by faith and patience, patience is one of the fruits of love. So, love is patience, and patience is love.

Mark 12:30-31 (NKJV) [30]And you shall love the Lord your God with your whole heart, with all your soul (your life), with all your mind (with your faculty of thought and your moral understanding), and with all your strength'. This *is* the first (and principal) commandment. [Deuteronomy 6:4-5]

[31]And the second, like *it, is* this: 'You shall love your neighbor as yourself.' There is no other commandment greater than these." [Leviticus 19:18]

We are commanded to love, without love one's faith is null and void. The Christian can only walk, run and fly in the things of the spirit by faith and love. Just as the eagle cannot fly only one wing, the eagle needs both wings to navigate through the storm, so the eagle Christian needs the both faith and love to navigates through the storms of life.

Galatians 5:6 [6]For [if we are] in Christ Jesus, neither circumcision nor uncircumcision counts for anything, but only faith activated and energized and expressed and working through love.

From Hebrews 6:12, the Bible says by faith and patience the elders obtain the promise, patience is the fruit of love so by faith and love they walked in the things of the spirit.

Mounting up with Wings:

During Isaiah's lifetime, the dispirited nation of Israel suffered a period of great distress politically as oppressive Assyrian powers invaded and conquered their lands. Isaiah chapters 40–48 contain promises of redemption and deliverance from the suffering. That section of the book starts with the words "Comfort, comfort my people, says your God" (Isaiah 40:1). Israel had nearly given up hope, thinking God had abandoned them, yet Isaiah drives his point home in Isaiah 40:27–31, "Why do you say, O Jacob, and speak, O Israel, 'My way is hidden from the Lord, and my right is disregarded by my God'? Have you not known? Have you not heard? The Lord is the everlasting God, the Creator of the ends of the earth. He does not faint or grow weary; his understanding is unsearchable. He gives power to the faint, and to him who has no might he increases strength. Even youths shall faint and be weary, and young men shall fall exhausted; but they who wait for the Lord shall renew their strength; they shall mount up with wings like eagles; they shall run and not be weary; they shall walk and not faint." (ESV).

Ancient Hebrew culture revered eagles as mighty warriors that also cared fiercely for their young. Eagles carry their eaglets to safety, away from the threat of predators. Eagles are also known for their strength and courage in dangerous, turbulent weather, soaring above storm clouds and to safety. Eagles' wings was a figure of speech commonly used to attribute these fine characteristics to a person. The Lord references eagles' wings in Exodus 19:1–6, which is a recollection of how God delivered Israel from the Egyptians. In this passage, the Lord gives Moses a message for His people:

"You yourselves have seen what I did to Egypt, and how I carried you on eagles' wings and brought you to myself. Now if you obey me fully and keep my covenant, then out of all nations you will be my treasured possession." (Verses 4–5).

The prophet Isaiah uses wings like eagles in the same way, attributing the great characteristics of eagles to those who remain faithful to God and look forward to their heavenly reward. The phrase mount up is a translation of the Hebrew word 'Allah', which means "to go up, ascend, to go up over a boundary." Isaiah is communicating the promise that God will provide renewed strength and courage to overcome obstacles if Israel would only have patience and trust in the Lord's sovereign timing.

Upon reading Isaiah's words, perhaps Israel recalled what God had said to them long ago as they fled Egypt, about how the Lord had delivered them "on eagles' wings" with His great strength and power. Isaiah tells them that they, too, could have access to such deliverance. If they remained faithful to God, they would soar.

Christians today can apply the principle of Isaiah 40:31 by trusting in God's sovereignty and waiting faithfully for Him. "We do not lose heart. Though outwardly we are wasting away, yet inwardly we are being renewed day by day."

2 Corinthians 4:16 [16]God in His grace will provide power, strength, and courage to the weary, weak, and downtrodden when they are willing to be patient and wait on Him. God will cause us to mount up on eagles' wings. So for you to grow and go deeper in the things of the spirit we must learn to wait upon God in prayer and fasting, and the studying and in meditating on the word of God.

CHAPTER 4

The Power of Faith

In the Bible the wings of an eagle signify the strength of God applied to us. Eagles are graceful birds, powerful and strong, flying and soaring above all; they are quite inspiring to look at. As we see them flying up in the sky, nothing seems to bother them or bind them; they are boundless, free. It takes strong wings for the eagle to fly in the sky and above the storm, so it takes a strong faith for the believer to walk victorious in the things of the spirit. We get faith and grow in faith by the hearing of the word of God, but strong faith comes by prayer and fasting, and also by praying in the Spirit. (Jude 20)

Jude 1:20 [20]But you, beloved, build yourselves up [founded] on your most holy faith [make progress, rise like an edifice higher and higher], praying in the Holy Spirit.

Faith Comes by Hearing the Word:

Romans 10:17 [17]So then faith *cometh* by hearing, and hearing by the word of God.

1 Peter 2:2 [2] (NKJV) As newborn babes, desire the sincere milk of the word, that ye may grow thereby: From the above scripture faith is developed by hearing the word of God, so faith is a product of the word of God. We receive and grow in faith by continuously hearing the word of God. For us to grow in faith we must desire the word of God as newborn babes. Just as newborn babes need milk in order to grow, we must desire the word of God so we can grow. The Bible did not say that faith comes praying, many people who wanted faith instead hearing the word, they rather resort to prayer. The more you hear the word of God the more you grow in faith and in spiritual things. It is the responsibility of every child of God to hear the word for himself in order to receive the faith he or she needs to receive the miracle he or she needs. Without the wings of faith, the eagle believer cannot fly.

Developing a Strong Wing of Faith:

Jude 1:20 [20]But you, beloved, build yourselves up [founded] on your most holy faith [make progress, rise like an edifice higher and higher], praying in the Holy Spirit; (AMP)

1 Corinthians 14:4 [4]He who speaks in a [strange] tongue edifies and improves himself, but he who prophesies [interpreting the divine will and purpose and teaching with inspiration] edifies and improves the church and promotes growth [in Christian wisdom, piety, holiness, and happiness]. (AMP)

To grow in faith and in spiritual things you need to hear the word of God more and more, and over and over. But to grow a strong wing of faith you must wait on the Lord and in prayer and fasting. Especially praying in the Holy Spirit.

The Bible says from the above scripture that building up yourselves in your most holy faith, prayer builds and strengthens your faith, prayer makes your faith strong to face challenges and to go through them and come out of them successfully.

Luke 22:31-32 [31] Simon, Simon (Peter), listen! Satan has asked excessively that [all of] you be given up to him [out of the power and keeping of God], that he might sift [all of] you like grain, [Job 1:6-12; Amos 9:9]

[32]But I have prayed especially for you (Peter), that your (own) faith

may not fail; and when you yourself have turned again, strengthen and establish your brethren. (AMP))

The Devil try to attack Peter, and Jesus saw it, and He told Peter about it, but surprisingly Jesus did not deliver Peter out of it but pray for him that his faith will be strong so that he can face the devil and overcome his temptation. Jesus prayed for Peter's faith to be strengthened, so prayer strengthens our faith. The more you pray the more your faith becomes strong, fear vanishes. the stronger the faith, the more ones get know the lord and the more they will do exploits.

Waiting Upon the Lord:

Isaiah 40:31 [31]But those who wait for the Lord [who expect, look for, and hope in Him] shall change and renew their strength and power; they shall lift their wings and mount up [close to God] as eagles [mount up to the sun]; they shall run and not be weary, they shall walk and not faint or become tired. [Hebrews 12:1-3]

The Eagle has the longest lifespan of its species. It can live up to 70 years. But to reach this age, the eagle must make a very difficult decision!

In its 40th year, the eagles long and flexible Talons can no longer grab a prey which serves as food. Its long and sharp beak becomes bent.

Its old-aged and heavy wings, due to their thick feathers, stick to its chest and make it difficult to fly. Then, the eagle is left with only two options: DIE or go through a painful process of CHANGE!

This process lasts for 150 days (Five months)

The process requires the eagle to fly to a mountain top and sit on its nest. There the eagle knocks its beak against a rock until it plucks it out. Then the eagle will wait for the new beak to grow back after which it will pluck out its talons. When its talons grow back, the eagle starts plucking its old aged feathers. And after this the eagle takes its famous flight of rebirth and LIVES for 30 more years!!

In order to survive and live. We too have to start the change process. We sometimes need to get rid of the unpleasant old memories, negative habits and our fixed mind set. Only Freed from the past burdens can we take advantage of the present.

If an eagle can make a lifesaving and life changing decision at the age of 40...why can't we? In order to take on a New Journey ahead, let go of your negative old limiting beliefs.

Open up your mind and let yourself fly high like an eagle!

When it rains, all birds occupy shelter. But the EAGLE avoids the rain by flying above the clouds...The problem is common to all but the attitude to solve it makes the difference!

Don't be afraid of change...accept it gracefully!!!

My questions to you is this! Do you want to fly with the eagles or scratch with the turkeys!! Over to you! The period of waiting upon the Lord in prayer and fasting is not an easy thing, but if you can go through, your strength will be renewed for the next part of your spiritual journey. When we wait upon the lord in prayer and fasting our faith and love is strengthened and renewed.

Putting Your Faith to Work:

Mark 5:25-29 [25]And there was a woman who had had a flow of blood for twelve years,

[26]And who had endured much suffering under [the hands of] many physicians and had spent all that she had and was no better but instead grew

worse.

[27]She had heard the reports concerning Jesus, and she came up behind Him in the throng and touched His garment,

[28]For she kept saying, If I only touch His garments, I shall be restored to health.

[29]And immediately her flow of blood was dried up at the source, and [suddenly] she felt in her body that she was healed of her [distressing] ailment.

Until you put your faith to work, your faith remains dead. The eagle is ready to release its wings to soar into greater heights. For the eagle Christian to fly in the spirit, and in signs and wonders, he or she must be ready to put his or her faith into action. From the above scripture the woman with the issue of blood released her faith into action and by her faith she was made whole.

CHAPTER 5

Power of Patience

Hebrews 6:12 In order that you may not grow disinterested and become [spiritual] sluggards, but imitators, behaving as do those who through faith (by their leaning of the entire personality on God in Christ in absolute trust and confidence in His power, wisdom, and goodness) and by practice of patient endurance and waiting are [now] inheriting the promises.

From the above scripture the writer of Hebrews writes that we should follow the way of life of those eagles (our predecessors), who had gone ahead of us in this faith. We should follow their faith and patient, which are the two wings of eagle Christian. So, from the above scripture, the first wing of the eagle Christian is faith, and second wing of the eagle Christian is patience which is an attribute of love.

The eagle is a bird of great patience, for the eagle to catch the right thermal to soar upon it can wait for days in order to catch the right wind before it soar. The eagle is very different from the other birds, the other birds flap their wings to fly, but the eagle stretches its wings in order to soar upon the wind. for the eagle to catch the right amount wind it needs to soar, a great deal of patience is needed here.

Catching a Prey:

James 1:4 [4]But let endurance and steadfastness and patience have full play and do a thorough work, so that you may be (people) perfectly and fully developed (with no defects), lacking in nothing.

For the eagle to catch it prey, it needs a great deal of patience. When the eagle spot a prey, the eagle will have enough patience and wait for the right time to strike that is why, it is hard for the eagle to miss its prey. If the eagle doesn't wait, it will lose its prey and will miss its target. It takes patience for the eagle to catch a prey. For the eagle Christian to receive a miracle from the Lord, the believer needs a great deal of patience, the Bible says by faith and patience Abraham and the eagles who have gone ahead of us inherited the promise by their faith and patience.

The Bible says in, Psalm 40:1-2

[1]I WAITED patiently and expectantly for the Lord; and He inclined to me and heard my cry.

[2]He drew me up out of a horrible pit [a pit of tumult and of destruction], out of the miry clay (froth and slime), and set my feet upon a rock, steadying my steps and establishing my goings.

David says from the above scripture that he waited patiently to receive the answer to his prayers. Any believe who cannot have patient and wait for the right to receive from God the will surely miss his or her miracle, the Bible says let patience have his perfect work. Anyone who does not have patience is like an eagle who is only flying on one wing, and that cannot fly in things in the things of the spirit. so, for the eagle Christian to receive what he or she desires it takes a great of patience and faith.

Patience is Endurance:

In the Bible patience means endurance, it is waiting on God and enjoying with anticipation or expectation. Patience means to endure to the expected end and not been worried about the circumstances. The eagle is a bird of endurance, whiles the eagle is waiting for the right time to launch out, it also endures the hardship of the storm, LOVE IS PATIENCE.

CHAPTER 6

The Training of the Eaglet

Deuteronomy 32:11-12 [11]As an eagle that stirs up her nest, that flutters over her young, He spread abroad His wings and He took them, He bore them on His opinions. [Luke 13:34]

[12]So the Lord alone led him; there was no foreign god with Him.

In the life development of the eaglet, learning how to fly and soar, and its subsequent training is the most interesting thing in the life of the eagle. The following the mother eagle goes through to raise her young ones.

- **Tenderness**

Strength, tenacity, a keen sense of vision, swiftness of flight, intelligence, loyalty, and many other celebrated attributes characterize eagles. Less commonly known, but equally notable, is the tenderness they show their young—a surprising characteristic for such fierce birds of prey.

Parent eagles invest in, nurture, and vigilantly watch over their young. During incubation, one parent remains in the nest at all times to provide warmth and protection for the developing eaglet. The other parent hunts, supplies provision, and keeps a watchful eye from nearby, a pattern that continues even after the eaglet hatches. Like a parent eagle tenderly meeting every need, so the Lord of hosts hovers over his people, protects us (Isaiah 31:5), provides for our every need (Philippians 4:19), and never, ever leaves or forsakes us (Deuteronomy 31:6).

Indeed, we are "the apple of his eye."

- **Imprinting**

As a young eagle grows, it learns from its parents by imprinting—a process in which an animal gains its sense of species identification. During a critical stage of development, eaglets will imprint to their parents, an object, or some other animal, and will identify with that species for life. Protection aside, this is another compelling reason eagle parents remain close: to faithfully demonstrate essential life skills and impart an appropriate sense of identity to their young.

God knew we would be inclined to imprint to this world and its broken ways (Ephesian. 2:1-10). He knew we needed a Savior, someone to show the way for those who are his. And so, he sent Jesus, who is the "radiance of the glory of God and the exact imprint of his nature" (Hebrews 1:3). Jesus perfectly demonstrated how to live and imparted to us an appropriate sense of identity as children of the living God.

- **Fledgling**

Early on the parent eagles cater to their eaglets' every need. Food is provided and shredded by the parents in the nest. This act not only provides sustenance, but also demonstrates how to use their beak and talons. As eaglets grow, parents gradually wean the eaglet from their aid to encourage the eaglet to develop essential survival skills.

Soon, food is no longer shredded and brought to the eaglet's beak, but instead is dropped farther away, encouraging the eaglet to move about the nest and develop its shredding skills. For short periods of time the eaglet is left alone, though a parent eagle is never far off. As the eaglets move around the empty nest, exploring or gathering food, the process of strengthening their wings begins.

Parent eagles then flutter over the nest, often with food just out of reach. Doing so not only demonstrates to the eaglets what their side appendages can do, but also compels the eaglets to flap those side appendages to grasp the food.

The awkward flapping of the wings and foraging strengthens the eaglet's wings, preparing her for flight. Similarly, God uses our struggles as a means to strengthen us. Our suffering produces endurance, character, and hope. (Romans 5:3) In his faithfulness to us, God prepares us to take flight.

- **Stirring the Nest**

Eventually, parent eagles return to the nest less frequently and with less food. When parents do return, they may thrash about removing the comforts lining the nest. Bewildered, frustrated, and confused the eaglet moves, branches out of the nest, and begins to test out her wings out of desperation.

Frustration, hunger, and discomfort are her parents' intentions. Persecution, problems, frustrations and hunger and discomfort are parts of God development plans for us. Without these conditions the baby Christian will not develop into the full fledge mature Christian that God wants he or she to be. The parents wisely know that without this disruptive environment their young will not grow, learn, and develop the essential skills for survival.

Though the eaglet does not understand this at the time, the lack of food and removal of comfort is an act of tender care and love, a gift of provision by her parents who know that without the ability to fly, she cannot survive and thrive. Unknown to the eaglet, the parents are giving her the gift of flight. . .the gift of life.

Faith for the Christian is like flight for an eagle: essential to survive and thrive. The eagle develops a strong wing to fly higher and through the process of despair and frustration and problems. Therefore, we as believers develops strong faith in Christ through the things we go through in life.

Often times we feel like an eaglet: striving, flapping, fledgling. Yet, as we flap, forage, and fledge our strength is given.

Much like the eaglet bewildered by her parents, we may be bewildered by our Father's actions (or lack thereof). We may even feel our Father has forgotten us, abandoned us, or withheld good from us.

Yet, as the Lord did for the Israelites in the desert, so he encircles us, he cares for us, he keeps us as the apple of his eye. Though it may feel painful, and confusing, in stirring our nest our heavenly Father is actually giving us the gift of life. . .the gift of faith. . .the gift of flight.

"But they who wait for the Lord shall renew their strength; they shall mount up with wings like eagles; they shall run and not be weary; they shall walk and not faint." Isaiah 40:31

Developing a Strong Strength of Faith:

Ephesians 6:10 [10]In conclusion, be strong in the Lord [be empowered through your union with Him]; draw your strength from Him [that strength which His boundless might provide].

As the strength of eagle is the wings, so the strength of the eagle Christian is in his or her wings, and the wings of the eagle Christian are faith and love (patience). So, how strong ones faith and love is show how strong the believer, from the above scripture the Bible says be strong, He did not say be weak. For the eagle to soar higher and higher above the storms, then its wings must be very strong. Without strength in the wings of the eagle of the eagles, the storm will carry it away, so likewise the believer need to have strength in his or her, so for the believer to soar higher and higher in the things of the spirit, he or she must be very strong in faith.

The following are the process of how to develop a strong faith:

- **Faith Comes Continual Hearing**

Romans 10:17 [17]So faith comes by hearing [what is told], and what is heard comes by the preaching [of the message that came from the lips] of Christ (the Messiah Himself).

One's faith grows stronger by continual hearing of the word of God.

- **Meditation**

Joshua 1:8 [8]This Book of the Law shall not depart out of your mouth, but you shall meditate on it day and night, that you may observe and do according to all that is written in it. For then you shall make your way prosperous, and then you shall deal wisely and have good success.

One's faith gets stronger, by daily meditating on the word of God, as one thinks over and over again on the word of God, one's faith grows stronger and stronger.

- **Prayer**

Jude 1:20 (NKJV) [20]But you, beloved, build yourselves up (founded) on your most holy faith (make progress, rise like an edifice higher and higher), praying in the Holy Spirit,

One of the spiritual exercises that builds the faith of the believer and makes it stronger is prayer, especially praying in the Spirit.

1 Corinthians 14:4 [4]He who speaks in a [strange] tongue edifies and improves himself, but he who prophesies [interpreting the divine will and purpose and teaching with inspiration] edifies and improves the church and promotes growth [in Christian wisdom, piety, holiness, and happiness].

The Bible says that he that prays in an unknown tongue edifies himself, that builds his faith and makes it stronger.

- **Putting Your Faith to Work**

James 2:17 [17]So also faith, if it does not have works (deeds and actions of obedience to back it up), by itself is destitute of power (inoperative, dead).

Any time you put your faith to work your faith grows and become more stronger, one of the major ways of growing your faith is by putting faith to work, the more you use your faith to solve problems, the more your faith grows and it becomes stronger. The Bible says that faith without works is dead, that means if you don't use your faith it will die, and it will grow weak.

Using Your Faith to Deal with Challenges:

1 Samuel 17:34-37 [34]And David said to Saul, Your servant kept his father's sheep. And when there came a lion or again a bear and took a lamb out of the flock,

[35]I went out after it and smote it and delivered the lamb out of its mouth; and when it arose against me, I caught it by its beard and smote it and killed it.

[36]Your servant killed both the lion and the bear; and this uncircumcised Philistine shall be like one of them, for he has defied the armies of the living God!

[37]David said, The Lord Who delivered me out of the paw of the lion and out of the paw of the bear, He will deliver me out of the hand of this Philistine. And Saul said to David, Go, and the Lord be with you!

One of the major reasons God allows challenges to come on our way is so that you can use your faith to solve them. Any time you use your faith to solve your problems, it boosts your confidence, and it takes your faith to next level. So, from the above scripture because David used his faith to deal with the lion and the bear, his faith graduated to the level of killing Goliath.

So, challenges are the marks of a champion, so the storm is the mark of an eagle.

So, the eaglet grows and matures into a full fledge eagle by the training that the mother eagle gives to it, and it develops a strong wings, sharp beak and strong claws for hunting its own food and preys. So, we as eagle Christians grow into full fledge sons and daughters of God, having strong faith and love (patience) to possess our blessings on daily bases, by the challenges that our Heavenly Father allows us to go through as His children.

The Eagle and the Storm:

1 Corinthians 10:13 For no temptation (no trial regarded as enticing to sin), [no matter how it comes or where it leads] has overtaken you and laid hold on you that is not common to man [that is, no temptation or trial has come to you that is beyond human resistance and that is not adjusted and adapted and belonging to human experience, and such as man can bear]. But God is faithful (to His Word and to His compassionate nature), and He (can be trusted) not to let you be tempted and tried and assayed beyond your ability and strength of resistance and power to endure, but with the temptation He will (always) also provide the way out (the means of escape to a landing place), that you may be capable and strong and powerful to bear up under it patiently.(AMP)

They love the storm...They use the pressure of the storm to glide higher without having to use their own energy. They are able to do this because God has created them uniquely with an ability to lock their wings in a fixed position in the midst of the fierce storm wind. The storm doesn't frighten them, they love and that is what makes them to soar higher and higher in the air. So likewise we Christians are eagles, and we are supposed to love the challenges of life, but not run away from them, just as the storm is what elevates the eagle, the challenges of are meant to elevates us, and not to bring us down, they are make us soar higher and higher in life. So, we must learn to take advantage of the challenges of life to our advantage, and not run from them.

CHAPTER 7

The Conclusion

Galatians 5:16 [16]But I say, walk and live (habitually) in the [Holy] Spirit (responsive to and controlled and guided by the Spirit); then you will certainly not gratify the cravings and desires of the flesh (of human nature without God).

As eagles soar higher and higher in the things of the spirit, so the believer who is a spiritual eagle who belongs to the spiritual realm, eagles belongs to the air, and we are to walk and live and soar in the spiritual realm permanently. So, from the above scriptures says that we are to walk, fly and live in the spirit permanently, that is where we belong and that is how we escape gratifying the desires of the flesh.

So, the means of we the believers living continually in the spirit is by living by faith and love of God consistently on daily bases, and that is how all our needs are met as eagles Christians and as children of the Most High God.

ABOUT THE AUTHOR

Bishop Emmanuel Ogba Okereke is the founder of the Faith Authority Chapel International, a growing and thriving ministry based in Accra, Ghana with branches. He is the president of Emmanuel Okereke Ministries that organizes various seminars in apostolic and prophetic revival programs, leadership, wealth creation, and marriage for the body of Christ. Bishop Emmanuel Ogba Okereke is a teacher, an apostle, a prophet, and also a businessman with a strong unction in the apostolic and prophetic ministry. His messages are centered on faith, righteousness, wealth creation, soul winning, marriage, and relationships.

He is the author of four books:
1. Power Leadership Quotes (Vol 1.)
2. The Pathway to Godly Success
3. The Fight of Faith
4. Winning the Gate of the Lost

Bishop Okereke is a conference speaker who has travelled around most of the African countries to preach the gospel of Jesus Christ. He has a passion for teaching and encouraging Christians to live a life of faith in the Lord Jesus Christ and ensuring that they reign in every area of their lives as

Christians. Bishop holds a master's degree in Divinity, a degree in Biblical Studies, and he is also a product of the COLLEGE OF AFRICAN PROFESSIONAL WRITERS' AND JOURNALISM. He is married and lives with his family in Accra, Ghana.

Below is Bishop's contact information, he would love to hear from you:

Email: okerekegm@gmail.com **or** ogbagm@gmail.com
For public engagement contact:
EMMANUEL OKEREKE MINISTRIES
(+233-208192938, 0541670577)

ABOUT THE BOOK

Flying on the Wings of the Eagle "The Christian Eagle"

The eagle is the only bird that represents the spiritual life of the believer. The eagle is the only bird that is ascribed to God. For God is an eagle and every true born-again believer is an eagle.

The lifestyle of the eagle represents the spiritual life of the believer. The believer has a lot of lessons to learn from how the eagle operates in the air. The flying of the eagle in the air represents the spiritual operations of the believer. The eagle soars higher than any other bird in the air. The eagle can soar higher above the clouds on two wings, and the strength and the ability of the eagle to soar higher above the clouds is in its wings.

Every born-again believer is an eagle and the believer has two wings just as the eagle. The believer's ability to operate in walking in the spiritual realms is based on his or her two wings. The two wings of the eagle Christian is his Love and Faith. This is what Bishop Emmanuel Ogba Okereke is trying to unravel in this book. **Flying on the Wings of the Eagle** "The Eagle Christian" has a lot of revelations concerning how the eagle Christian can be successful in his or her spiritual life and walk.

The Bible says in Isaiah 40:31:

[31]But those who wait for the Lord (who expect, look for, and hope in Him) shall change and renew their strength and power; they shall lift their wings and mount up (close to God) as eagles [mount up to the sun]; they shall run and not be weary, they shall walk and not faint or become tired. [Heb. 12:1-3]

THIS IS A MUST-READ BOOK FOR EVERY CHRISTIAN BELIEVER, BECAUSE IT WILL TEACH YOU HOW TO BE A SUCCESSFUL IN YOUR SPIRITUAL LIFE.

www.ingramcontent.com/pod-product-compliance
Lightning Source LLC
Chambersburg PA
CBHW052120070526
44584CB00017B/2577